dachshund

understanding and
caring for your breed

D1100734

Written by
Jennifer Lowe

dachshund

understanding and caring for your breed

Written by
Jennifer Lowe

Pet Book Publishing Company

Bishton Farm, Bishton Lane, Chepstow, NP16 7LG, United Kingdom.
St Martin's Farm, Zeals, Warminster, BA12 6PD United Kingdom

Printed by Printworks Global Ltd., London & Hong Kong

Every reasonable care has been taken in the compilation of this
publication. The Publisher and Author cannot accept liability for any
loss, damage, injury or death resulting from the keeping of Dachshunds
by user(s) of this publication, or from the use of any materials,
equipment, methods or information recommended in this publication
or from any errors or omissions that may be found in the text of this
publication or that may occur at a future date, except as expressly
provided by law.

The 'he' pronoun is used throughout this book instead of the rather
impersonal 'it', however no gender bias is intended.

ISBN: 978-1-906305-78-9
ISBN: 1-906305-78-1

Acknowledgements

The publishers would like to thank the following for help with
photography: Ian and Sue Seath (Sunsong), Zena Thorn Andrews
(Drakesleat), Jason Hunt (Carpaccio), Carole Worswick (Dolyharp).

|Contents

Introducing
the Dachshund

The Dachshund is a breed like no other, with his 'sausage dog' conformation and his temperament – a remarkable combination of fearless hunter and faithful companion. Added to that, there are six varieties to choose from.

When you first look at a Dachshund, you think that a dog of this shape and size could never serve a useful purpose. But you would be quite wrong. The Dachshund is designed to go down a hole and dig and, when you look at him, that makes sense. His role was to locate badgers and, as well as needing an outstanding sense of smell to find them, he also needed great courage to dig them out.

Although there are still Dachshunds that are used for tracking and hunting, the breed has evolved to become one of the most popular companion dogs. He is highly adaptable, and his bold, outgoing

temperament makes him a dog that suits a variety of owners. You can even choose a size to suit your lifestyle!

Physical characteristics

The Dachshund comes in two sizes: standard and miniature. The varieties are identical in every aspect except size – the miniature is simply a smaller, more refined version.

The Dachshund is a small dog, with an elongated body that is close to the ground. He has short legs and big paws. His front legs are particularly powerful as these were used for digging. The line of the body ends with a tail that is carried with a slight upward curve. The tail was used as marker by huntsmen, and the upward curve meant that they could spot dogs when they were working in thick undergrowth, or were half-way down a hole.

The Dachshund has a most striking head, and this is enhanced by the bold, defiant, head carriage, which is so typical of the breed. The head is framed by drop ears, and the eyes convey keenness and intelligence.

Not only can you choose the size of Dachshund you want, you can also choose the coat type. Dachshunds may be smooth-haired, long-haired or wire-haired and each variety has its ardent enthusiasts. The

smooths look sleek and elegant, the long-hairs give a softer and sweeter impression, and the wire-hairs, with their bristling eyebrows and beard, look most impressive.

The miniature variety is a down-sized version of the standard.

When it comes to colors, you are spoilt for choice. There are solid colors (all one color), two colors (solid colors with tan or cream markings), dapples (merle pattern), brindles (striped pattern) and sables (dark overlay on red).

Scenthounds

The Dachshund is classified in the Hound group, which relates to his hunting ancestry. The group is divided into hounds that hunt by sight, such as Greyhounds, Afghan Hounds and Salukis, and hounds that hunt by scent. The Dachshund, along with breeds such as the Basset Hound, the Bloodhound and the Beagle, are classed as scenthounds.

Temperament

The Dachshund has a wonderful temperament; it combines many different facets, but they all add up to make a great companion dog.

The Breed Standard, which describes the 'perfect' Dachshund, gives an excellent account of his character. There are different versions of the Standard depending on national governing bodies, but the Dachshund is variously described as:

- **Clever:** He is quick to size up a situation and has the ability to use his own initiative.

- **Lively:** He has lots of energy and loves to join in with all activities.

- **Courageous to the point of rashness:** This comes from his hunting ancestry, going underground and confronting an animal such as a badger.

Facing page:
The Dachshund
temperament is second
to none.

- **Persevering:** This applies to his tracking skills – once a Dachshund is on a scent, he will be deaf to your calls.

- **Obedient:** With positive training, the Dachshund is ready and willing to co-operate, and can also take part in some of the canine sports.

- **Friendly:** With his outgoing temperament, the Dachshund is ready to greet everyone as his friend.

- **Faithful:** He is a most devoted companion.

- **Versatile:** This is a dog that will adapt to a variety of lifestyles.

- **Passionate:** An unusual adjective to describe a dog, but it sums up the Dachshund's wholehearted attitude to life.

- **Good tempered:** Every day is a good day for the Dachshund...

Companion dog

The Dachshund is happy in most situations – urban or rural, apartment or mansion, families with children or older owners. His adaptability is his greatest asset. As long as he is given sufficient exercise and mental stimulation, and is not left on his own for lengthy periods, he will be content.

If you have very small children, it may be better to delay getting a Dachshund until they are a little older. But generally the Dachshund will be a lively playmate as long as mutual respect is established on both sides.

A Dachshund will lead a fulfilling life as a single dog, but they are very sociable and enjoy the company of other dogs. As working dogs they were kept in packs; they have a natural way of relating to their own kind, and can often form strong attachments.

Life expectancy

The Dachshund was developed to be a hardy, hunting dog, and if he is bred without exaggeration, and given the correct care, he will enjoy a good life expectancy. Most dogs will reach their early teens, and some do even better. Dachshunds reaching 15 years and over are not unusual.

Tracing back in time

Dogs with long bodies and short legs have been documented for centuries; there is even evidence from ancient Egypt of this type of hunting dog. But we need to fast forward to the 18th century to find the origins of the Dachshund that we know today.

The name Dachshund means 'badger hound' in German – and Germany is the breed's native home. Dogs were needed to work underground in pursuit of badger, and so larger hunting dogs, such as the Bracke (a type of Bloodhound), the German Shorthaired Pointer, and the Pinscher were selectively bred to produce a small, long-bodied hunter.

Known as the Dackel or Teckel (a name still used for working dogs), these small dogs hunted by scent, working their way through thick undergrowth to find wild boar and badger. They hunted in packs and were completely fearless; dogs were prepared to dig their way into a badger's den and confront this most formidable of opponents. The Dachshund's job was to chase the badger from its den and then corner it until the hunters arrived.

Soon it was decided that the Dachshund could be used on rabbit and fox if he was small enough to get down the holes leading to the burrow or earth.

The smaller Teckels were selected and crossed with toy terriers or pinschers to establish a miniature variety, which became highly valued members of the hunting party.

Broadening horizons

The first Dachshunds reached the UK in 1840 when Queen Victoria's consort, Prince Albert, received a gift of a number of smooth-hairs from Prince Edward of Saxe Weimar. They were kept at Windsor and took part in pheasant shoots. Prince Albert introduced Queen Victoria to the new breed, and she was enchanted.

From then onwards, Dachshunds always numbered among her dogs. When her beloved Dachshund, Dacko, died at the age of 12, she wrote in a letter:

"I am greatly distressed at my dear old 'Dacko' having died. The dear old dog was so attached to me and had such funny, amusing ways, with large melancholy expressive eyes, and was quite a part of my daily life, always in my room, and I will miss him very much..."

Queen Victoria did much to popularize Dachshunds in the UK; they were exhibited at dog shows from 1866, where they were named as German Badger Dogs in classes for Foreign Sporting Dogs. A growing number of imports were brought in from Germany to strengthen the gene pool.

It was not long before the Dachshund made its mark in the USA, although the breed was imported for some years before gaining official recognition. The Dachshund Club of America was founded in 1881, and four years later a black and tan dog called Dash, owned by Dr G.D. Stewart, became the first Dachshund to be registered with the American Kennel Club.

Developing the breed

Initially it was the smooth-haired Dachshund that formed the foundation of the breed in its homeland, and when it spread overseas. But then it was the turn of the wire-hairs and the long-hairs.

Wire-hairs

There is evidence of wire-haired Dachshunds dating back to the 18th century; the wire coat was probably a throwback to the wire-haired pinschers which were used in the development of the breed. However, wire-haired Dachshunds were few in number and did not gain in popularity until the foundation of the German Teckel Klub in Germany in 1888. Soon after, a wire-hair called Mordax was exhibited at a show in Berlin and won first prize.

English horse dealers, who came looking for new stock in Germany, introduced terriers to mate with

the smooth-hairs and it was decided that the Dandie Dinmont was the best cross. The wire-hair gradually became established, and has always been highly valued as a working dog because his tough, wiry coat allowed him to work in the thickest undergrowth.

The miniature wire-hair was the last of the six varieties to be recognized; they were bred down from standard-sized dogs, and some miniature smooths were also used to achieve the desired result.

Long-hairs

This variety may have arisen by selectively breeding smooth-haired Dachshunds that had slightly longer coats, but it is more likely that the German Stoberhund, and some of the spaniel breeds, were introduced. Certainly, the early photos of long-hairs look very spaniel-like.

The breed in the UK was based on German imports, and after a long-hair won at Crufts in 1923, this variety became increasingly popular. In the USA, long-hairs were kept mainly as pets, and it was not until 1931 that the first long-haired Dachshund was registered with the American Kennel Club.

The miniature variety was developed by breeding long-hairs with drop-eared Papillons, known as Phalenes. However, it took many years of dedicated breeding before the miniature long-hair achieved the true Dachshund look.

The breed today

From its beginnings in Germany, the Dachshund has become a worldwide favorite. It is valued as a distinctive show dog and a loyal companion, and the working dogs – Teckels – are highly sought after for their tracking skills. In the USA, the Dachshund is ranked in the top ten of most popular breeds.

Long-haired Dachshunds bear a strong resemblance to Spaniels, which were used in their development.

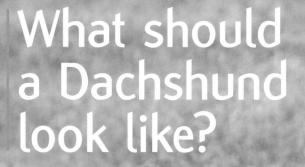

What should a Dachshund look like?

There can be no mistaking a Dachshund, with his moderately-long body, short legs, and a head that is carried with boldness and defiance. He is first and foremost a sporting breed, and although the vast majority of Dachshunds are kept as companion dogs, he should still resemble a working dog, ready and able to do a day's work.

The aim of breeders is to produce dogs that are sound, healthy, typical examples of their chosen breed in terms of both looks and temperament. To achieve this, they are guided by a Breed Standard, which is a written blueprint describing what the perfect specimen should look like. For the purposes of the Breed Standard, the six Dachshund varieties are treated as one breed, but with specific guidance on size and coat type.

Of course, there is no such thing as a 'perfect' dog, but breeders aspire to produce dogs that conform as closely as possible to the picture in words presented by the Breed Standard. In the show ring, judges use

Points of anatomy

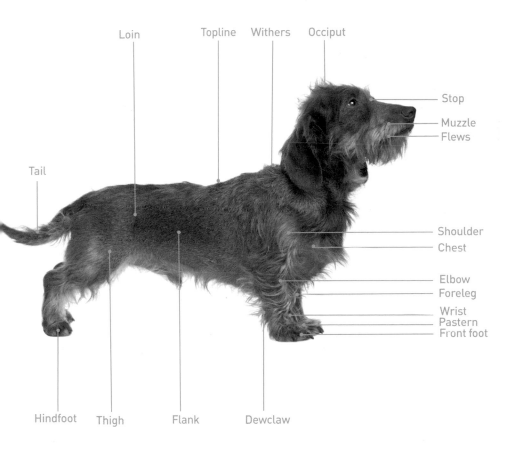

Loin

Topline　Withers　Occiput

Stop

Muzzle
Flews

Tail

Shoulder
Chest

Elbow
Foreleg

Wrist
Pastern
Front foot

Hindfoot　Thigh　Flank　Dewclaw

the Breed Standard to assess the dogs that come before them, and it is the dog that, in their opinion, comes closest to the ideal, that will win top honors.

This has significance beyond the sport of showing for it is the dogs that win in the ring that will be used for breeding. The winners of today are therefore responsible for passing on their genes to future generations and preserving the breed in its best form.

There are some differences in Breed Standards depending on national Kennel Clubs. The American Standard is more descriptive than the English version. The Federation Cynologique International, which is the governing body for 86 countries, including Germany, also provides a highly detailed and informative Standard.

General appearance

Long and low to the ground, the Dachshund is short in the leg, but has robust muscular development. The height at the wither (the highest point of the shoulder) should be half the length of the body. Despite his short legs, the Dachshund should be mobile and lithe. It is therefore important that he is well balanced and without exaggeration which could hamper his capacity for movement. The UK Standard states: "Essential that functional build is retained to ensure working ability".

The Dachshund is characterized by his bold, defiant head carriage and his intelligent expression.

Temperament

The Dachshund temperament is a wonderful mixture of courageous hunter and good-tempered companion. He is friendly and obedient, with no sign of nervousness or shyness.

Head and skull

Viewed from above, or the side, the head tapers to the tip of the nose and is conical in shape. The skull is slightly arched, and in the wire-haired variety it is a little broader. It slopes gradually, without a prominent stop (the indentation between the muzzle and the forehead) into a slightly arched muzzle. The American Standard describes this as a "Roman appearance".

The nose leather is well developed and the nostrils are open, which befits a dog that is bred to be a scenthound. The lips are described variously as "taut" and "well stretched" covering powerful jaws.

Eyes

The eyes are almond-shaped and medium in size. They are set obliquely in the skull, and convey a sense of alertness and intelligence. They should be dark-colored, except in chocolates, where they may be lighter. In dapples one or both eyes may be blue, known as 'wall' eyes.

Ears

The ears are set on high, but they should not be carried too far forward. They should be of moderate length and rounded. When a Dachshund is animated, the forward edge of the ears will touch the cheek, framing the face.

Mouth

Bred to be a hunter, the Dachshund must have powerful jaws and well-developed teeth. The correct dentition is a scissor bite, with the teeth on the upper jaw closely overlapping the teeth on the lower jaw.

Neck

The neck is long and muscular, and is crucial in giving the Dachshund his defiant head carriage. It should be slightly arched, running in graceful lines to the shoulders. There should be no evidence of dewlap (loose skin beneath the lower jaw).

Forequarters

In order to work underground, the Dachshund must have powerful forequarters, with long broad shoulder blades placed obliquely (45 degrees to the

Facing page: The eyes are dark with an intelligent expression.

horizontal) upon a robust ribcage. Viewed from the front, the powerful forelegs should fit closely to the forechest, but not so close as to impede movement.

Ground clearance is an important consideration, and it is an area where exaggeration can creep in. At its lowest point between the forelegs, the chest should be halfway between the elbow and the wrist.

Body

The body is long and muscled. When viewed in profile, the back should lie in the "straightest possible line" between the withers and the short, slightly arched loin (the waist, just behind the ribcage). Although the body must be long, moderation is important; if it is too long the back will be weak with associated health risks. Again, sufficient ground clearance should be considered essential.

Hindquarters

The rear assembly provides the driving force when a Dachshund is moving and therefore it must be muscular and well angulated. From the rear, the thighs are strong and powerful and the hindlegs should be perfectly parallel to each other.

Feet

The feet are a Dachshund speciality and seem massive in proportion to the leg. They are designed for digging, with strong well-arched toes which are close together. The nails are strong, and the pads are thick and firm. The hind feet are slightly smaller and narrower than the front feet.

Tail

This should continue the line of the spine, and there should be a slight curve. The tail should not be carried gaily (over the back).

Gait/movement

The Dachshund should move with a free and flowing stride, covering the ground with ease. The front legs should reach forward without too much lift and operate in unison with the driving action of the hind legs.

Coat

The Breed Standard gives descriptions of the three coat types:

Smooth: This coat is short, dense and shining. The hair on the underside of the tail is coarse in texture. The skin should be loose and supple, with little or no wrinkle.

Long: Soft and sleek, the coat may have a slight wave. On the body it should lie flat so as not to obscure the outline. The hair is longer under the neck, along the undercarriage and behind the legs. There is profuse feathering on the ears and tail.

Wire: With the exception of the jaw, eyebrows and ears, the whole body is covered with a short, thick, hard textured outer coat, with a finer, softer undercoat. The facial features form distinguished bushy eyebrows and beard; in contrast, the hair on the ears is almost smooth. The legs and feet are neatly furnished with harsh coat, and the tail is evenly covered with close-fitting hair.

Color

Dachshunds come in a wide range of colors and markings; in all varieties, dogs with large patches of white are not acceptable.

The following colors and markings are permitted:

Whole-color: Red or cream, with or without shading of dark hairs.

Two colors: Black, chocolate, wild boar, grey (blue) and fawn, also known as Isabella. Each color has rich tan or cream markings.

Facing page:
1. Wire-hair colors (left to right): Chocolate and tan, brindle (wild boar), black and tan, grey brindle.
2. Smooth dapple.
3. Long-haired red.
4. Smooth black and tan.

Dappled: A merle pattern expressed as lighter colored areas contrasting with the darker base color, which may be any of the acceptable colors.

Brindle: A pattern of black or dark stripes over the entire body.

Sable: A pattern that consists of a uniform dark overlay on red dogs.

In wire-haired Dachshunds, all the colors listed above are allowed, but the most common are wild boar (an agouti pattern formed by banded hairs), black and tan, chocolate and various shades of red.

Size

In the USA and the UK, size is calculated in terms of weight, which is divided into standard and miniature. The American Breed Standard stipulates a wide range of 16-32lb (7-14kg) for standards; the British go for a smaller range of 20-26lb (9-12kg). American miniatures are shown in classes for dogs that are under 11lb at 12 months of age and older; the ideal weight for a British miniature is given as 10lb (4.5kg).

In countries governed by the FCI, the chest circumference is measured as a means of determining the correct size. This dates back to the Dachshund's working ancestry, where the circumference of the chest equaled the hole the

Dachshund could go down. There are three categories in FCI countries: standard, and miniature, which is sub-divided into rabbit and the smaller dwarf.

Summing up

Although the majority of Dachshunds are pet dogs and will never be exhibited in the show ring, it is important that breeders strive for perfection and try to produce dogs that adhere as closely as possible to the Breed Standard. The emphasis is on breeding dogs that are capable of fulfilling their original function as hunting dogs, working underground. Most Dachshunds will not be called on to do this, but having the correct conformation – and guarding against exaggeration – ensures that the breed remains fit and healthy. Dachshunds must be able to lead active, fulfilling lives.

The aim is to breed typical, healthy Dachshunds that are sound in body and mind.

What do you want from your Dachshund?

There are hundreds of dog breeds to choose from, so how can you be sure that the Dachshund is the right breed for you? Before you take the plunge into Dachshund ownership, weigh up the pros and cons so you can be 100 per cent confident that this is the breed that is best suited to your lifestyle.

Companion

The Dachshund originally comes from working stock but, for most dogs, this part of his history is firmly in the past, and it is in the role of companion that the Dachshund excels. He is a natural fit in a family, and he thrives on being part of a busy household. He takes a keen interest in everything that is going

on, and will be self-appointed guard of your home. In fact, the Dachshund is a very friendly dog, and welcomes visitors, but he likes to give warning. A Dachshund's bark is deep and sonorous, and gives the impression of a far bigger dog.

No doubt you have studied the Dachshund temperament in some detail, and the description in the Breed Standard applies to all varieties. However, owners agree that there are some minor differences which may influence your choice. The consensus is that standard wire-hairs are the most active and extrovert, standard longs are the most laid back, and standard smooths are more 'one person or 'one family' dogs. Miniatures are sweet-natured, less demanding in terms of exercise, and ideally suited to owners with less active lifestyles.

There is one further point that should be considered. The Dachshund bonds closely with his family, and this is particularly true of miniatures, but you do not want your Dachshund to become too dependent. If you dog has not been trained to spend time alone, he may become anxious, feeling that he has been deserted. This is very distressing for both dog and owner, and can reach a point where a dog barks constantly when he is left, or even becomes destructive. To prevent this happening, accustom your puppy to spending short periods on his own –

ideally when he is safe and secure in an indoor crate – and he will understand that although you go away, you always come back.

Show dog

Do you have ambitions to exhibit your Dachshund in the show ring? This is a specialist sport, which often becomes highly addictive, but you must have the right dog to start with.

If you plan to show your Dachshund, you need to track down a show quality puppy, and train him so he will perform in the show ring, and accept the detailed 'hands on' examination that he will be subjected to when he is being judged.

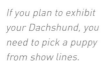

If you plan to exhibit your Dachshund, you need to pick a puppy from show lines.

Show presentation is very important, and the workload, and expertise required, depends on the coat type. Smooths are the most straightforward, longs need extensive grooming, and wires are high maintenance – the choice is yours.

It is also important to bear in mind that not every puppy with show potential develops into a top-quality specimen, so you must be prepared to love your Dachshund and give him a home for life, even if he doesn't make the grade.

Working dog

The Dachshund's original role of hunting badger and wild boar is now defunct, but there are working dogs, known as Teckels, that still work for a living. Their role is to keep down vermin, and they also perform a very useful task on country estates, tracking fallen deer. If you are interested in this aspect of Dachshund ownership, you will need to go to a breeder who specializes in working lines.

Sports dog

The intelligent Dachshund is more than capable of advanced training, and will enjoy the challenge of some of the canine sports. Obviously you need to find a sport that suits his conformation, but the Dachshund is very versatile, and with positive training, he will always be prepared to have a go.

For more information on dog sports, see page 152.

Facing page: The Dachshund retains strong working instincts.

What does your Dachshund want from you?

A dog cannot speak for himself, so we need to view the world from a canine perspective and work out what a Dachshund needs in order to live a happy, contented and fulfilling life.

Time and commitment

First of all, a Dachshund needs a commitment that you will care for him for the duration of his life – guiding him through his puppyhood, enjoying his adulthood, and being there for him in his later years. If all potential owners were prepared to make this pledge, there would be scarcely any dogs in rescue.

The Dachshund's primary role is to be a companion dog, and this is what he must be. If you cannot give your Dachshund the time and commitment he deserves, you would be strongly advised to delay owning a dog until your circumstances change.

Practical matters

The Dachshund is an adaptable dog and will cope with varying amounts of exercise. However, it is important to bear in mind that standards need considerably more exercise than miniatures. A standard has the energy and endurance to enjoy long treks, but he will cope with shorter outings, particularly if there is an element of variety. Miniatures may not require so much exercise, but their needs should not be neglected. A miniature is still a hound at heart and will relish the opportunity to use his nose and explore new places.

When it comes to grooming, you need to choose your

variety with care, as the workload varies greatly: smooth (minimal), long-hair (medium care), wire-hair (needs a professional groomer).

For more information on grooming, see page 108.

Mental stimulation

The mistake that many owners make is thinking that a small dog does not need to be trained. This is a disaster with almost any breed, but particularly so with the Dachshund which is a hound, bred to use his brain and to take the initiative.

A well-trained Dachshund is a joy to own, but you cannot leave this highly intelligent dog to his own devices. Although he doesn't have an ounce of malice in his make up, a Dachshund who is allowed to rule the roost is not fun to live with. He will become very demanding – and if doesn't get what he wants, he may bark at you until you give in.

As a responsible owner, you must give your dog a sense of leadership so he is happy to accept you as the decision maker in the family. You must channel his energy and his intelligence. It does not matter what you do with him – training exercises, teaching tricks, trips out in the car, or going for new, interesting walks – all are equally appreciated, and will give your Dachshund a purpose in life.

Extra considerations

Now you have decided that a Dachshund is the dog for you, and you have worked out the variety you want, you can narrow your choice still further so you know exactly what you are looking for.

Color

There is a brilliant array of colors to choose from, and all Dachshund enthusiasts have their favorites. Generally, the choice is narrower in wire-hairs, with wild boar, chocolate and red being most readily available.

Take great care if your preference is for a dapple Dachshund. The pattern is very attractive, but you will need to do some extra research on the breeding stock. Puppies born from mating dapple to dapple – known as double dapples – have a high risk of developing conditions such as congenital deafness and blindness. In the UK, the Kennel Club will not register puppies from these matings.

Male or female?

The decision as to whether you opt for a male or female really does come down to personal preference. In some breeds, the male is a bigger animal, but in Dachshunds the only difference is whether you choose a standard or a miniature.

Some owners reckon that females are more loving and affectionate, but owners of males would swear the opposite! They would claim that males may be more independent but they are also more loyal. The only certainty is that all dogs are individuals, and you can never second-guess how your Dachshund is going to turn out.

You may find a female slightly more difficult to care for as you will need to cope with her seasonal cycle, which will start around six to nine months of age, with seasons occurring every six months or so thereafter. During the three-week period of a season, you will need to keep your female away from entire males (males that have not been neutered) to eliminate the risk of an unwanted pregnancy. Some owners report that their female Dachshunds become a little moody or withdrawn in the time leading up to, and during, a season.

Neutering puts an end to the seasons, and also has many attendant health benefits. The operation, known as spaying, is usually carried out at some point after the first season. The best plan is to seek advice from your vet.

An entire male may not cause many problems, although some do have a stronger tendency to mark, which could include the house. However, training will usually put a stop to this. An entire male will also be on the lookout for females in season, and this may lead to difficulties, depending on your circumstances.

Neutering (castrating) a male is a relatively simple operation, and there are associated health benefits. Again, you should seek advice from your vet.

More than one?

Dachshunds are sociable dogs and certainly enjoy each other's company. But you would be wise to guard against the temptation of getting two puppies of similar ages, or two from the same litter.

Unfortunately there are some unscrupulous breeders who encourage people to do this, but they are thinking purely in terms of profit, and not considering the welfare of the puppies.

Looking after one puppy is hard work, but taking on two pups at the same time is more than double the workload. House training is a nightmare as, often, you don't even know which puppy is making mistakes, and training is impossible unless you separate the two puppies and give them one-on-one attention.

The puppies will never be bored as they have each other to play with. However, the likelihood is that the pair will form a close bond, and you will come a poor second.

If you do decide to add to your Dachshund population, wait at least 12-18 months so your first dog is fully trained and settled before taking on a puppy. The best advice is to get dogs of opposite sexes. Although this will mean that you need to neuter one, or both dogs, the male-female relationship seems to work far better.

Acquiring two puppies of a similar age can be a recipe for disaster.

An older dog

You may decide to miss out on the puppy phase and take on an older dog instead. Such a dog may be harder to track down, but sometimes a breeder may have a youngster that is not suitable for showing, but is perfect for a family pet. In some cases, a breeder may rehome a female when her breeding career is at an end so she will enjoy the benefits of getting more individual attention.

There are advantages to taking on an older dog, as you know exactly what you are getting. But the upheaval of changing homes can be quite upsetting, so you will need to have plenty of patience during the settling in period.

Rehoming a rescued dog

We are fortunate that the number of Dachshunds that end up in rescue is relatively small, and this is often through no fault of the dog. The reasons are various, ranging from illness or death of the original owner to family breakdown, changing jobs, or even the arrival of a new baby.

It is unlikely that you will find a Dachshund in an all breed rescue centre, but the specialist breed clubs run rescue schemes, and this will be your best option if you decide to go down this route.

Try to find out as much as you can about a dog's history so you know exactly what you are taking on. You need to be realistic about what you are capable of achieving so you can be sure you can give the dog in question a permanent home.

Again, you need to give a rescued Dachshund plenty of time and patience as he settles into his new home, but if all goes well, you will have the reward of knowing that you have given your dog a second chance.

Do you feel able to give a Dachshund a second chance of finding a forever home?

Sourcing a puppy

Your aim is to find a healthy puppy that is typical of the breed, and has been reared with the greatest possible care. Where do you start?

A tried-and-trusted method of finding a puppy is to attend a dog show where your chosen breed is being exhibited. This will give you the opportunity to see Dachshunds of all varieties. To begin with, the dogs of each variety look very similar, although you will see different colors, but when you get your eye in you will see subtle differences.

This is because breeders produce dogs with a family likeness and seeing a number of dogs in the ring will give you the opportunity to gauge which type you prefer.

When judging has been completed, talk to the exhibitors and find out more about their dogs. They may not have puppies available, but some will be planning a litter, and you may decide to put your name on a waiting list.

Internet research

The Internet is an excellent resource, but when it comes to finding a puppy, use it with care:

DO go to the website of your national Kennel Club.

Both the American Kennel Club (AKC) and the Kennel Club (KC) have excellent websites which will give you information about the Dachshund as a breed, and what to look for when choosing a puppy. You will also find contact details for specialist breed clubs (see opposite).

Both sites have lists of puppies available, and you can look out for breeders of merit (AKC) and assured breeders (KC) which indicates that a code of conduct has been adhered to.

DO find details of specialist breed clubs.

On breed club websites you will find lots of useful information that will help you to care for your Dachshund. There may be contact details of breeders in your area, or you may need to go through the club secretary. Some websites also have a list of breeders that have puppies available. The advantage of going through a breed club is that members will follow a code of ethics, and this will give you some guarantees regarding breeding stock and health checks.

DO NOT look at puppies for sale online.

There are legitimate Dachshund breeders with their own websites, and they may, occasionally, advertise a litter, although in most cases reputable breeders have waiting lists for their puppies.

The danger comes from unscrupulous breeders that produce puppies purely for profit, with no thought for the health of the dogs they breed from and no care given to rearing the litter. Photos of puppies are hard to resist, but never make a decision based purely on an advertisement. You need to find out who the breeder is, and have the opportunity to visit their premises and inspect the litter before making a decision.

Questions, questions, questions

When you find a breeder with puppies available, you will have lots of questions to ask. These should include the following:

- Where have the puppies been reared? Hopefully, they will be in a home environment, which gives them the best possible start in life.

- How many are in the litter?

- What colors are they?

- What is the split of males and females?

- How many have already been spoken for? The breeder will probably be keeping a puppy to show or for breeding, and there may be a number of potential purchasers on a waiting list.

- Can I see the mother with her puppies? The answer to this should always be 'yes' – even if the breeder is in the process of weaning the puppies, you should still be given the opportunity to see mother and pups together.

- What age are the puppies?

- When will they be ready to go to their new homes?

Bear in mind puppies need to be with their mother and siblings until they are eight weeks of age, otherwise they miss out on vital learning and communication skills which will have a detrimental effect on them for the rest of their lives.

You should also be prepared to answer a number of searching questions so the breeder can check if you are suitable as a potential owner of one of their precious puppies.

You will be asked some or all of the following questions:

- What is your home set up?

- Do you have children/grandchildren?

- What are their ages?

- Is there somebody at home the majority of the time?

A caring breeder will welcome your questions.

- Have you considered the costs involved in coat care for this breed?

- What is your previous experience with dogs?

- Do you have plans to show your Dachshund?

The breeder is not being intrusive; they need to understand the type of home you will be able to provide in order to make the right match. Do not be offended by this; the breeder is doing it for both the dog and for your benefit, too. Be very wary of a breeder who does not ask you questions. He or she may be more interested in making money out of the puppies rather than ensuring that they go to good homes. They may also have taken other short cuts which may prove disastrous in terms of vet bills or plain heartache.

Health issues

In common with all purebred dogs, the Dachshund suffers from a few hereditary problems. The most significant affect the back (see page 188), but most hereditary conditions relate to the eyes. In order to try to eliminate these from the breed, an annual eye examination can be carried out, and this should this should be considered essential for breeding stock.

For more information on breed specific conditions, see page 182.

Facing page: Find out about the health status of the puppies' parents.

Puppy
watching

Puppies are irresistible, and Dachshund pups are no exception. When you look at a litter you will be entranced; each pup seems to have his own very individual character. But this is a situation where you must not let your heart rule your head. You are making a long-term commitment, so you need to be 100 per cent confident that the breeding stock is healthy, and the puppies have been reared with love and care.

Viewing a litter

It is a good idea to have mental checklist of what to look out for when you visit a breeder. You want to see:

- A clean, hygienic environment.

- Puppies that are out-going and friendly, and eager to meet you.

- A sweet-natured mother who is ready to show off her babies.

- Puppies that are well covered, but not pot-bellied, which could be an indication of worms.

- Coats should look clean and healthy, with no sign of scurf or sore patches.

- Bright eyes, with no sign of soreness or discharge.

- Clean ears that smell fresh.

- No discharge from the nose.

- Clean rear ends – matting could indicate upset tummies.

- Lively pups who are keen to play.

It is important that you see the mother with her puppies, as this will give you a good idea of the temperament they are likely to inherit. It is also helpful if you can meet other close relatives so you can see the type of Dachshund the breeder produces.

In most cases, you will not be able to see the father (sire) as most breeders will travel some distance to find a stud dog that is not too close to their own bloodlines and complements their bitch. However, you should be able to see photos of him and be given the chance to examine his pedigree and show record.

Companion puppy

If you are looking for a Dachshund as a companion, you should be guided by the breeder, who will have spent hours and hours puppy watching, and will know each of the pups as individuals. It is tempting to choose a puppy yourself, but the breeder will take into account your family set up and lifestyle and will help you to pick the most suitable puppy.

Show puppy

If you are buying a puppy with the hope of showing him, make sure you make this clear to the breeder. A lot of planning goes into producing a litter, and although all the puppies will have been reared with equal care, there will be one or two that have show potential.

Ideally, recruit a breed expert to inspect the puppies with you, so you have the benefit of an objective evaluation. The breeder will also help with your choice as they will want to ensure that only the best of their stock is exhibited in the show ring. Look out for a puppy with the following attributes:

- A head of the correct conical shape. The eyes should be almond-shaped and dark in color. They may be lighter in chocolate colored Dachshunds, and in dapples one or both eyes may be blue.

Facing page: Be completely honest with the breeder so they can help you to choose the most suitable puppy.

- The body should be that of an adult in miniature with a level topline and a tail that follows the line of the back.

- The forechest is visible but not fully developed.

- Good angulation fore and rear to give a balanced appearance.

- The correct scissor bite, with the teeth on the upper jaw closely overlapping the teeth on the lower jaw. This can change as a puppy develops, so this can only be a guideline.

- An extrovert, out-going temperament.

Coats are hard to assess at this stage as all Dachshund puppies are born with smooth coats. In long-hairs the feathering appears gradually; it is reckoned that the pups that look almost smooth until late in puppyhood, develop the best coats.

Wires will show a trace of beard, and they will have some longer, coarser hairs on the body, legs and in between the toes. There are two types of wire coat: the classic wire and the pin wire which, at this stage, looks completely smooth. When the adult coat comes through, it is similar to the classic wire coat, but the facial furnishings are minimal. The advantage of this coat is that it may not need stripping. For more information, see page110.

Bear in mind that puppies change as they mature.

Remember, there are no guarantees, and if your Dachshund fails to make the grade in the show ring, he will still be an outstanding companion and a much-loved member of your family.

A Dachshund-friendly home

It may seem an age before your Dachshund puppy is ready to leave the breeder and move to his new home. But you can fill the time by getting your home ready, and buying the equipment you will need.

In the home

The Dachshund is a great explorer and will be on the lookout for anything that appears new and interesting. If you add in a puppy's natural curiosity, you will see that your house is the equivalent of one big playground. Of course, you want your puppy to have fun, but the top priority is to keep him safe.

The best plan is to decide which rooms your Dachshund will have access to, and make these areas puppy friendly. Trailing electric cables are a major hazard and these will need to be secured out of reach. You will need

to make sure all cupboards are secure, particularly in the kitchen where you may store cleaning materials that could be toxic to dogs. Household plants can also be poisonous, so these will need to relocated, along with breakable ornaments.

The Dachshund's elongated conformation means that he is vulnerable while he is growing, and so you will need to prevent him from negotiating stairs. The best way of doing this is to use a baby gate, making sure your puppy cannot squeeze through, which could result in injury.

In the garden

The Dachshund will not leap over boundary fences – but he will dig. This means that he can find his way out very easily if there are gaps under fencing or if he burrows under hedges. You therefore need to inspect all boundaries for possible escape routes. Gates leading from the garden should also be checked to ensure they have secure fastenings.

If you are a keen gardener, you may want to protect your prized plants from unwanted attention. Some owners allocate a specific area of the garden as a 'digging patch', which keeps everyone happy. Bear in mind that there are a number of flowers and shrubs that are toxic to dogs, so check this out on the Internet (a list is available at www.dogbooksonline.

co.uk/caring/poisonous-plants/) or by seeking advice from your local garden center.

You will also need to designate a toileting area. This will assist the house-training process, and it will also make cleaning up easier. For information on house-training, see page 96.

House rules

Before your puppy comes home, hold a family conference to decide on the house rules. For example, is your Dachshund going to be allowed to roam downstairs, or will you keep him in the kitchen unless you can supervise him elsewhere? When he is in the sitting room, is he allowed to come on your lap for a cuddle?

These are personal choices, but once you have allowed your puppy to do something, he will think that this is 'allowed', regardless of whether you change your mind. You and your family must make decisions – and stick with them – otherwise your puppy will be upset and confused, not understanding what you want of him.

There is another consideration: a Dachshund should not be allowed to jump on and off furniture, which could be harmful to his back. If are going to allow your Dachshund on the sofa or the armchair, you must be there to help him on and off.

Buying equipment

There are some essential items of equipment you will need for your Dachshund. If you choose wisely, much of it will last for many years to come.

Indoor crate

Rearing a puppy is so much easier if you invest in an indoor crate. It provides a safe haven for your puppy at night, when you have to go out during the day, and at other times when you cannot supervise him. A puppy needs a base where he feels safe and secure, and where he can rest undisturbed. An indoor crate provides the perfect den, and many adults continue to use them throughout their lives. It is therefore important to buy a crate that is large enough for your Dachshund when he is fully grown.

You will also need to consider where you are going to locate the crate. The kitchen is usually the most suitable place as this is the hub of family life. Try to find a snug corner where the puppy can rest when he wants to, but where he can also see what is going on around him, and still be with the family.

Beds and bedding

The crate will need to be lined with bedding and the best type to buy is synthetic fleece. This is warm and cozy, and as moisture soaks through it, your puppy will not have a wet bed when he is tiny and is still unable to go through the night without relieving himself. This type of bedding is machine washable and easy to dry. Buy two pieces, so you have one to use while the other piece is in the wash.

If you have purchased a crate, you may not feel the need to buy an extra bed, although many Dachshunds like to have a bed in the family room so they feel part of household activities. There is an amazing array of dog-beds to chose from – duvets, bean bags, cushions, baskets, igloos, mini-four posters – so you can take your pick! Before you make a major investment, wait until your puppy has gone through the chewing phase; you will be surprised at how much damage can be inflicted by small teeth.

Collar and leash

You may think that it is not worth buying a collar for the first few weeks, but the sooner your pup gets used to it, the better. All you need is a lightweight puppy collar; you can buy something more exotic when your Dachshund is fully grown.

A nylon leash is suitable for early leash training, but make sure the fastening is secure. Again, you can invest in a more expensive leash at a later date – there are lots of attractive collar and leash sets to choose from.

ID

Your Dachshund needs to wear some form of ID when he is out in public places. This can be in form of a disc, engraved with your contact details, attached to the collar. When your Dachshund is full-grown, you can buy an embroidered collar with your contact details, which eliminates the danger of the disc becoming detached from the collar.

You may also wish to consider a permanent form of ID. Increasingly breeders get puppies micro-chipped before they go to their new homes. A micro-chip is the size of a grain of rice. It is 'injected' by a vet under the dig's skin, usually between the shoulder blades, with a special needle. It has some tiny barbs on it, which dig into the tissue around where it lies, so it does not migrate from that spot.

Each chip has its own unique identification number which can only be read by a special scanner. That ID number is then registered on a national database with your name and details, so that if ever your dog is lost, he can be taken to any vet or rescue centre where he is scanned and then you are contacted.

Bowls

Your Dachshund will need two bowls; one for food, and one for fresh drinking water, which should always be readily available. A stainless steel bowl is a good choice for food as it is tough and hygienic. Plastic bowls may be chewed, and there is a danger that bacteria can collect in the small cracks that may appear.

You can opt for a second stainless steel bowl for drinking water, or you may prefer a heavier ceramic bowl which will not be knocked over so easily.

Food

The breeder will let you know what your puppy is eating and should provide a full diet sheet to guide you through the first six months of your puppy's feeding regime. How much they are eating per meal? How many meals per day? When to increase the amounts given per meal and when to reduce the meals per day.

The breeder should provide you with some food when you go and collect your puppy, but it is worth making enquiries in advance about the availability of the brand that is recommended.

Grooming equipment

This will depend on your Dachshund's coat. All that is needed for the smooth-coat is a hound glove. Both longs and wires need a good-quality bristle brush and a wide-toothed steel comb for the longer hair and feathers. A slicker brush is useful for getting out mats and tangles from long-haired Dachshunds.

In addition, you should buy nail clippers, a toothbrush, and toothpaste that is specially formulated for dogs.

Toys

The Dachshund can be surprisingly destructive, so soft, squeaky toys are best avoided. The more robust toys, such as tug toys, and hard rubber kongs, are ideal. A kong can also be stuffed full of food, and this will give your Dachshund an occupation when he has to be left on his own.

A puppy can be very destructive so keep a close check on toys for damage.

It is important to get into the habit of checking toys on a regular basis for signs of wear and tear. If your puppy swallows a chunk of rubber or plastic, it could cause an internal blockage. This could involve costly surgery to remove the offending item, or at worst, it could prove fatal.

Finding a vet

Before your puppy arrives home, you should register with a vet. Speak to other pet owners that you might know, to see who they recommend. It is so important to find a good vet, almost as vital as finding a good doctor for yourself. You need to find someone with whom you can build up a good rapport and have complete faith in. Word of mouth is really the best recommendation.

When you contact a veterinary practice, find out the following:

- Does the surgery run an appointment system?

- What are the arrangements for emergency, out of hours cover?

- Do any of the vets in the practice have experience treating Dachshunds?

- What facilities are available at the practice?

If you are satisfied with what your find, and the staff appear to be helpful and friendly, book an appointment so your puppy can have a health check a couple of days after you collect him.

Settling in

When you first arrive home with your puppy, be careful not to overwhelm him. You and your family are hugely excited, but the puppy is in a completely strange environment with new sounds, smells and sights, which is a daunting experience, even for the boldest of pups.

The majority of Dachshund puppies are very confident: exploring their new surroundings, wanting to play straightaway and quickly making friends. Others need a little longer to find their feet. Keep a close check on your puppy's body language and reactions so you can proceed at a pace he is comfortable with.

First, let him explore the garden. He will probably need to relieve himself after the journey home, so take him to the allocated toileting area and, when he performs, give him plenty of praise.

When you take your puppy indoors, let him investigate again. Show him his crate, and encourage him to go in by throwing in a treat. Let him have a sniff, and allow him to go in and out as he wants to. Later on, when he is tired, you can put him in the crate while you stay in the room. In this way he will learn to settle and will not think he is being abandoned.

It is a good idea to feed your puppy in his crate, at least to begin with, as this helps to build up a positive association. It will not be long before your Dachshund sees his crate as his own special den and will go there as a matter of choice. Some owners place a blanket over the crate, covering the back and sides, so that it is even more cozy and den-like.

Meeting the family

Resist the temptation of inviting friends and neighbors to come and meet the new arrival; your puppy needs to focus on getting to know his new family for the first few days. Try not to swamp your Dachshund with too much attention; there will be plenty of time for cuddles later on!

If you have children in the family, you need to keep everything as calm as possible. Your puppy may not have met children before, and even if he has, he will still find them strange and unpredictable. A puppy can easily become alarmed by too much noise, or he may go to the opposite extreme and become over-excited, which can lead to mouthing and nipping.

The best plan is to get the children to sit on the floor and give them all a treat. Each child can then call the puppy, stroke him, and offer a treat. In this way the puppy is making the decisions rather than being forced into interactions he may find stressful.

If he tries to nip or mouth, make sure there is a toy at the ready, so his attention can be diverted to something he is allowed to bite. If you do this consistently, he will learn to inhibit his desire to mouth when he is interacting with people.

Right from the start, impose a rule that the children are not allowed to pick up or carry the puppy. They can cuddle him when they are sitting on the floor. This may sound a little severe, but a wriggly puppy can be dropped in an instant, sometimes with disastrous consequences

Involve all family members with the day-to-day care of your puppy; this will enable the bond to develop with the whole family as opposed to just one person. Encourage the children to train and reward the puppy, teaching him to follow their commands without question.

The animal family

Dachshunds are sociable and enjoy the company of other dogs, but make sure you supervise early interactions so relations with the resident dog get off on a good footing.

Your adult dog may be allowed to meet the puppy at the breeder's, which is ideal as the older dog will not feel threatened if he is away from home. But if this is not possible, allow your dog to smell the puppy's bedding (the bedding supplied by the breeder is fine) before they actually meet so he familiarizes himself with the puppy's scent.

The garden is the best place for introducing the puppy, as the adult will regard it as neutral territory. He will probably take a great interest in the puppy and sniff him all over. Most puppies are naturally submissive in this situation, and your pup may lick the other dog's mouth or roll over on to his back. Try not to interfere as this is the natural way that dogs get to know each other.

You will only need to intervene if the older dog is too boisterous, and alarms the puppy. In this case, it is a good idea to put the adult on his lead so you have some measure of control.

It rarely takes long for an adult to accept a puppy, particularly if you make a big fuss of the older dog so that he still feels special. However, do not take any risks and supervise all interactions for the first few weeks. If you do need to leave the dogs alone, always make sure your puppy is safe in his crate.

Meeting a cat should be supervised in a similar way, but do not allow your puppy to be rough as the cat may retaliate using its sharp claws. A Dachshund puppy may get over excited by the sight of a new furry friend, and may try to chase it. Make sure you stop this straightaway before bad habits develop. The best way to do this is to keep distracting your

puppy by calling him to you and offering him treats. In this way, he will switch his focus from the cat to you, and you can reward him for his 'good' behavior.

Generally, the canine-feline relationship should not cause any serious problems. Indeed, many Dachshunds count the family cat among their best friends.

Feeding

The breeder will generally provide enough food for the first few days so the puppy does not have to cope with a change in diet – and possible digestive upset – along with all the stress of moving home.

Some puppies polish off their food from the first meal onwards, others are more concerned by their new surroundings and are too distracted to eat.

Do not worry unduly if your puppy seems disinterested in his food for the first day or so. Give him 10 minutes to eat what he wants and then remove the leftovers and start afresh at the next meal.

Do not make the mistake of trying to tempt his appetite with tasty treats or you will end up with a faddy feeder. This is a mistake made by many Dachshund owners, and a scenario can develop where the dog holds out, refusing to eat his food, in the hope that something better will be offered.

Obviously if you have any concerns about your puppy in the first few days, seek advice from your vet.

The first night

Your puppy will have spent the first weeks of his life with his mother, or curled up with his siblings. He is then taken from everything he knows as familiar, lavished with attention by his new family – and then comes bed time when he is left all alone. It is little wonder that he feels abandoned.

The best plan is to establish a night-time routine, and then stick to it so that your puppy knows what is expected of him. Take your puppy out into the garden to relieve himself, and then settle him in his crate.

Some people leave a low light on for the puppy at night for the first week, others have tried a radio as company or a ticking clock. A covered hot-water bottle, filled with warm water, can also be a comfort. Like people, puppies are all individuals and what works for one, does not necessarily work for another, so it is a matter of trial and error.

Be very positive when you leave your puppy on his own – do not linger, or keep returning; this will only make the situation more difficult. It is inevitable that he will protest to begin with, but if you stick to your routine, he will accept that he gets left at night – but you always return in the morning.

Rescued dogs

Settling an older, rescued dog in the home is very similar to a puppy in as much as you will need to make the same preparations regarding his homecoming. As with a puppy, an older dog will need you to be consistent, so start as you mean to go on.

There is often an initial honeymoon period when you bring a rescued dog home, and he will be on his best behavior for the first few weeks. It is after this that the true nature of the dog will show, so be prepared for subtle changes in his behavior. It may be advisable to register with a reputable training club, so you can seek advice on any training or behavioral issues at an early stage.

Above all, remember that a rescued dog ceases to be a rescued dog the moment he enters his forever home and should be treated normally like any other family pet.

It is inevitable that your puppy will feel lonely for the first few nights.

House training

This is an aspect of training that most first-time puppy owners dread, but it should not be a problem as long as you are prepared to put in the time and effort.

Some breeders start the house-training process by providing the litter with paper or training pads so they learn to keep their sleeping quarters clean. This is a step in the right direction, but most pet owners want their puppies to toilet outside.

As discussed earlier, you will have allocated a toileting area in your garden when preparing for your puppy's homecoming. You need to take your puppy to this area every time he needs to relieve himself, so he builds up an association and knows why you have brought him out to the garden.

Establish a routine and make sure you take your

puppy out at the following times:

- First thing in the morning

- After mealtimes

- On waking

- Following a play session

- Last thing at night.

A puppy should be taken out to relieve himself every two hours as an absolute minimum. If you can manage an hourly trip out, so much the better. The more often your puppy gets it 'right', the quicker he will learn to be clean in the house. It helps if you use a verbal cue, such as "Busy", when your pup is performing and, in time, this will trigger the desired response.

Do not be tempted to put your puppy out on the doorstep in the hope that he will toilet on his own. Most pups simply sit there, waiting to get back inside the house! No matter how bad the weather is, accompany your puppy and give him lots of praise when he performs correctly.

Do not rush back inside as soon as he has finished. Your puppy might start to delay in the hope of prolonging his time outside with you. Praise him, have a quick game, then you can both return indoors.

When accidents happen

No matter how vigilant you are, there are bound to be accidents. If you witness the accident, take your puppy outside immediately, and give him lots of praise if he finishes his business out there.

If you are not there when he has an accident, do not scold him when you discover what has happened. He will not remember what he has done and will not understand why you are cross with him. Simply clean it up and resolve to be more vigilant next time.

Make sure you use a deodorizer, available in pet stores, when you clean up, otherwise your pup will be drawn to the smell and may be tempted to use the same spot again.

A lapse in house training is nearly always due to your lack of vigilance...

Choosing a
diet

There are so many different types of dog food on sale, all claiming to be the best – so how do you know what is likely to suit your Dachshund? This is a breed that can easily become overweight so you need to find a well-balanced diet that is suited to your dog's individual requirements.

When choosing a diet, there are basically three categories to choose from:

Complete

This is probably the most popular diet as it is easy to feed and is specially formulated with all the nutrients your dog needs. This means that you should not add any supplements or you may upset the nutritional balance.

Most complete diets come in different life stages: puppy, adult maintenance and senior, so this means that your Dachshund is getting what he needs when he is growing, during adulthood, and as he becomes older. You can even get prescription diets for dogs with particular health issues.

There are many different brands to choose from,

so seek advice from your puppy's breeder, who will have lengthy experience of feeding Dachshunds.

Canned/pouches

This type of food is usually fed with hard biscuit, and most Dachshunds find it very appetizing. However, the ingredients – and the nutritional value – do vary significantly between the different brands, so you will need to check the label. This type of food often has a high moisture content, so you need to be sure your Dachshund is getting all the nutrition he needs.

Homemade

There are some owners who like to prepare meals especially for their dogs – and it is probably much appreciated. The danger is that although the food is tasty, and your Dachshund may appreciate the variety, you cannot be sure that it has the correct nutritional balance.

If this is a route you want to go down, you will need to find out the exact ratio of fats, carbohydrates, proteins, minerals and vitamins that are needed, which is quite an undertaking.

The Barf (Biologically Appropriate Raw Food) diet is another, more natural approach to feeding. Dogs are fed a diet mimicking what they would have eaten in the wild, consisting of raw meat, bone, muscle, fat, and vegetable matter. This can be labor intensive if you buy all the ingredients yourself, but there are now pre-packed versions available from specialist stockists.

Feeding regime

When your puppy arrives in his new home he will need four meals, evenly spaced throughout the day. You may decide to keep to the diet recommended by your puppy's breeder, and if your pup is thriving there is no need to change. However, if your puppy is not doing well on the food, or you have problems with supply, you will need to make a change.

When switching diets, it is very important to do it on a gradual basis, changing over from one food to the next, a little at a time, and spreading the transition over a week to 10 days. This will avoid the risk of digestive upset.

When your puppy is around 12 weeks, you can cut out one of his meals; he may well have started to leave some of his food indicating he is ready to do this. By six months, he can move on to two meals a day – a regime that will suit him for the rest of his life.

Bones and chews

Puppies love to chew, and many adult dogs also

Facing page: Stick to a regime of two meals a day for the adult Dachshund.

enjoy gnawing on a bone. Bones should always be hard and uncooked; rib bones and poultry bones should be avoided, as they can splinter and cause major problems. Dental chews, and some of the manufactured rawhide chews, are safe, but they should only be given under supervision.

Ideal weight

The Dachshund may have short legs, but this does not mean that his stomach should be touching the ground! Dachshund owners seem to struggle more than most to keep their dogs at the correct weight, but it is of vital importance.

An obese dog may suffer from a number of serious health problems, which can have a major effect on life expectancy. Quality of life will also be affected, as an overweight Dachshund will become progressively less mobile and will not be able to exercise properly.

The Dachshund has perfected the art of looking at you with his dark, melting eyes telling you he is 'starving'. You will therefore need to harden your heart and think of your dog's figure! If you are using treats for training, remember to take these into account and reduce the amount you feed at his next meal.

When you are assessing your dog's weight, look

at him from above, and make sure you can see a definite 'waist' behind the ribcage. You should be able to feel his ribs, but not see them. When looking at his underside, there should be good ground clearance and a slight tuck up should be visible when he is viewed from the side.

In order to keep a close check on your Dachshund's weight, get into the habit of visiting your veterinary surgery on a monthly basis so that you can weigh him. You can keep a record of his weight so you can make adjustments if necessary.

If you are concerned that your Dachshund is putting on too much weight – or appears to be losing weight – consult your vet, who will give you advice and help you to plan a suitable diet.

Caring for your Dachsund

The Dachshund is a relatively easy breed to care for, particularly if you get the right balance between food intake and exercise so your dog remains fit and active. Coat care is dependent on the variety you have chosen.

Smooth coats

This is a very low-maintenance coat as it does not shed. All it needs is a weekly groom with a hound glove; some owners prefer to use a soft bristle brush, but either are fine. If you want to bring out the shine on the coat, you can give your Dachshund a 'polish' with a chamois leather. There are a number of lotions on the market which enhance the sheen in the coat, and these can also be used.

Long coats

This coat is soft in texture; it may be straight or have a slight wave. To keep it looking its best, regular brushing and combing is needed as mats and tangles form very easily. Grooming can be a lengthy process if you do not do it on a regular basis – at least every other day is recommended. Start getting your puppy used to being groomed from an early age and then he will learn to relax and enjoy the procedure

A bristle brush can be used on the body coat, but a slicker brush is required for the featherings. Work through the feathering, behind the ears where mats form, on the chest, the legs and underside. The feathering on the tail will need particular attention. Once you have groomed all the featherings with a slicker bush you need to start again, this time using a wide-toothed metal comb. There are a number of products you can buy which ease the process of grooming and help to keep the coat in good condition.

Wire coats

Wire-haired Dachshunds have a double coat, which consists of a dense undercoat and a harsh, wiry topcoat. The topcoat is tight fitting on the body, with longer hair on the legs, underside and the facial furnishings, which consist of eyebrows and a beard.

The body coat can be kept in good order with a bristle brush, but the longer hair will need to be combed to prevent matting. Debris, particularly food, can collect in the beard, so this must be kept clean and should be combed to prevent mats and tangles forming.

The wire coat does not shed like other coats; there may be minimal shedding, but not to the same extent as smooth or long-haired Dachshunds. However, the wire coat does need to be hand stripped two or three times a year. In the show world the process of hand stripping – taking out the dead hair using a stripping knife – is ongoing, gradually working to enhance the dog's shape and outline.

Pet owners generally opt to use a professional groomer and the coat will be stripped in one session. Clipping is incorrect for wire-coated Dachshunds as it ruins the harsh texture of the coat.

Some wire-haired Dachshunds are born with a 'pin wire' coat, and this will not need stripping. A typical pin wire has little or no face furnishings, but still has a double coat. The undercoat is dense and the topcoat is harsh, but is generally shorter than the classic wire-haired coat. Pin wire coats can be maintained very easily with a stiff bristle brush.

Bathing

There is no need to bath your dog on a regular basis, as it will have an adverse effect on the coat. However, Dachshunds do have a tendency to roll, particularly if they can find something especially smelly. On these occasions, there is no option but to bath your dog. Use a shampoo that is specially formulated for dogs, and rinse thoroughly to make sure no trace remains in the coat.

Routine care

In addition to grooming, you will need to carry out some routine care.

Eyes

Check the eyes for signs of soreness or discharge. You can use a piece of cotton (cotton-wool) – a separate piece for each eye – and wipe away any debris.

The smooth-haired Dachshund needs minimal coat care.

The workload steps up with long-hairs

Wire-haired Dachshunds need to have their coats stripped.

Ears

The ears should be clean and free from odor. You can buy specially-manufactured ear wipes, or you can use a piece of cotton (cotton-wool) to clean them if necessary. Do not probe into the ear canal or you risk damaging it.

With long- and wire-haired Dachshunds, you may find that hair grows inside the ears and can be a source of problems if it is not removed. This is most easily done using finger and thumb. The process is made simpler if you use an ear powder; the hair comes out more easily and causes less distress. Start doing this from an early age, rewarding your puppy for his co-operation, so he learns to accept it without fuss.

Teeth

Dental disease is becoming more prevalent among dogs so teeth cleaning should be seen as an essential part of your care regime. The build-up of tartar on the teeth can result in tooth decay, gum infection and bad breath, and if it is allowed to accumulate, you may have no option but to get your dog's teeth cleaned under anesthetic.

When your Dachshund is still a puppy, accustom him to teeth cleaning so it becomes a matter of routine.

Use a wad of cotton (cotton-wool) to clean the ears.

Teeth need attention on a routine basis.

Accustom your Dachshund to nail trimming from an early age.

Dog toothpaste comes in a variety of meaty flavors, which your Dachshund will like, so you can start by putting some toothpaste on your finger and gently rubbing his teeth. You can then progress to using a finger brush or a toothbrush, whichever you find most convenient.

Remember to reward your Dachshund when he co-operates and then he will positively look forward to his teeth-cleaning sessions.

Feet

Nail trimming is a task dreaded by many owners – and many dogs – but, again, if you start early on, your Dachshund will get used to the procedure.

Dark nails are harder to trim than white nails as you cannot see the quick (the vein that runs through the nail), which will bleed if it is nicked. The best policy is to trim little and often so the nails don't grow too long, and you do not risk cutting too much and catching the quick.

If you are worried about trimming your Dachshund's nails, go to your vet so you can see it done properly. If you are still concerned, you can always use the services of a professional groomer.

If you have a long-haired or wire-haired Dachshund, you will also need to inspect the pads on a regular basis. Long hair grows between the pads, and this needs to be trimmed. If it is neglected, the hair grows too long and becomes matted, which will be very uncomfortable for your dog.

Exercise

The Dachshund was bred to be a working hound and will need regular, varied exercise. Going for walks gives a dog the opportunity to use his nose and investigate new sights and smells. Dachshunds have an excellent sense of smell, and an opportunity to explore new places will be viewed as a great treat even if you do not go for miles.

Beware of over-exercising puppies as this can cause damage, such as out-turned feet, a poor topline, and poor body development. Exercise should be suited to a puppy's age, starting with playing in the garden, gradually increasing to five minute walks when he has completed his inoculations, 10 minute walks at four months, 15-20 minutes at five months, and 25-30 minutes at six months. By the time your Dachshund is 12 months of age, he will enjoy walks of around 45 minutes on a daily basis.

Back problems

The Dachshund's elongated conformation means there is an increased risk of back problems (see

Intervertebral Disc Disease, page 188). Good management will help to prevent problems arising, so all Dachshund owners should:

- Provide regular exercise

- Prevent the use of stairs wherever possible.

- Use a ramp when your Dachshund is getting in and out of the car.

- Stop your Dachshund jumping on or off furniture

- Always lift a Dachshund using both hands – one to support his chest, the other to support his back.

The older dachshund

We are fortunate the Dachshund has a good life expectancy, and you will not notice any significant changes in your dog until he reaches double figures, or maybe even later.

The older Dachshund will sleep more, and he may be reluctant to go for longer walks. He may show signs of stiffness when he gets up from his bed, but these generally ease when he starts moving. Some older Dachshunds may have impaired vision, and some may become a little deaf, but as long as their senses do not deteriorate dramatically, this is something older dogs learn to live with.

If you treat your older Dachshund with kindness and

Facing page:
Dachshunds thrive on
exercise – whatever the
weather!

consideration, he will enjoy his later years and suffer the minimum of discomfort. It is advisable to switch him over to a senior diet, which is more suited to his needs, and you may need to adjust the quantity, as he will not be burning up the calories as he did when he was younger and more energetic. Make sure his sleeping quarters are warm and free from drafts, and, if he gets wet, make sure you dry him thoroughly.

Most important of all, be guided by your Dachshund. He will have good days when he feels up to going for a walk, and other days when he would prefer to potter in the garden. If you have a younger dog at home, this may well stimulate your Dachshund to take more of an interest in what is going on, but make sure he is not pestered as he needs to rest undisturbed when he is tired.

Letting go

inevitably there comes a time when your Dachshund is not enjoying a good quality of life, and you need to make the painful decision to let him go. We would all wish that our dogs passed, painlessly, in their sleep but, unfortunately, this is rarely the case.

However, we can allow our dogs to die with dignity, and to suffer as a little as possible, and this should be our way of saying thank you for the wonderful companionship they have given us.

When you feel the time is drawing close, talk to your vet who will be able to make an objective assessment of your Dachshund's condition and will help you to make the right decision.

This is the hardest thing you will ever have to do as a dog owner, and it is only natural to grieve for your beloved Dachshund. But eventually, you will be able to look back on the happy memories of times spent together, and this will bring much comfort. You may, in time, feel that your life is not complete without a Dachshund and you will feel ready to welcome a new puppy into your home.

Try to put your dog's needs first at the end of his life.

Social skills

To live in the modern world, without fear and anxieties, a Dachshund needs to receive an education in social skills so that he learns to cope calmly and confidently in a wide variety of situations.

Early learning

The breeder will have started a program of socialization by getting the puppies used to all the sights and sounds of a busy household. You need to continue this, making sure your pup is not worried by household equipment, such the vacuum cleaner or the washing machine, and that he gets used to unexpected noises from the radio and television.

It is also important to handle your puppy on a regular basis so he will accept grooming and other routine care, and will not be worried if he has to be examined by the vet.

To begin with, your puppy needs to get used to all the members of his new family, but then you should give him the opportunity to meet friends and other people that come to the house.

Right from the start, teach him acceptable greeting behavior in the following way:

- Have treats at the ready, and once your puppy has said his first 'hello', distract his attention by calling him to you, giving him a treat and praising him.

- Let him return to the visitor (hopefully not barking), and then call him back to you for a treat and praise. In this way, the pup learns that coming to you is more rewarding than barking.

- Now give the visitor a couple of treats so that when your puppy approaches – and is not barking – he can be rewarded.

This training may take a bit of practice, but it is well worth persevering; the alternative is to invest in some earplugs!

It is also very important that your puppy learns to interact with children. If you do not have children, make sure your puppy has the chance to meet and play with other people's children so he learns that humans come in small sizes, too.

The outside world

When your puppy has completed his vaccinations, he is ready to venture into the outside world. Dachshund puppies take a lively interest in anything new and will relish the opportunity to broaden their horizons. However, there is a lot for a small puppy to take on board, so do not swamp him with too many new experiences when you first set out.

The best plan is to start in a quiet area with light traffic, and only progress to a busier place when your puppy is ready. There is so much to see and hear – people (maybe carrying bags or umbrellas), pushchairs, bicycles, cars, trucks, machinery – so give your puppy a chance to take it all in.

If he does appear worried, do not fall into the trap of sympathizing with him, or worse still, picking him up. This will only teach your pup that he had a good reason to be worried and, with luck, you will 'rescue' him if he feels scared.

Instead, give a little space so he does not have to confront whatever he is frightened of, and distract him with a few treats. Then encourage him to walk past, using a calm, no-nonsense approach. Your pup will take the lead from you, and will realize there is nothing to fear.

Your pup also needs to continue his education in canine manners, stared by his mother and by his littermates, as he needs to be able to greet all dogs

calmly, giving the signals that say he is friendly and offers no threat. If you have a friend who has a dog of sound temperament, this is an ideal beginning. As your puppy gets older and more established, you can widen his circle of canine acquaintances.

A well-socialized Dachshund will take the world in his stride.

Training classes

A training class will give your Dachshund the opportunity to interact with other dogs, and he will also learn to focus on you in a different, distracting environment.

Before you go along with your puppy, it is worth attending a class as an observer to make sure you are happy with what goes on.

Find out the following:

- How much training experience do the instructors have?

- Are the classes divided into appropriate age categories?

- Do the instructors have experience training Dachshunds?

- Do they use positive, reward-based training methods?

- Does the club train for the Good Citizen Scheme? See page 152.

If the training class is well run, it is certainly worth attending. Both you and your Dachshund will learn useful training exercises; it will increase his social skills, and you will have the chance to talk to lots of like-minded dog enthusiasts.

Training
guidelines

The Dachshund is a highly intelligent dog and he is generally eager to please. However, he does have a strong will and this can make him stubborn if training becomes monotonous, or if he lacks motivation.

Although you will be keen to get started, do not neglect the fundamentals in training that could make the difference between success and failure.

Try to observe the following guidelines:

- Choose an area that is free from distractions so your puppy will focus on you. You can move on to a more challenging environment as your pup progresses.

- Do not train your puppy just after he has eaten or when you have returned from exercise. He will either be too full, or too tired, to concentrate.

- Do not train if you are in a bad mood, or if you are short of time – these sessions always end in disaster!

- Make sure you have a reward your Dachshund values – tasty treats, such as cheese or cooked liver, or an extra special toy.

- If you are using treats, make sure they are bite-size, otherwise you will lose momentum when your pup stops to chew on his treat.

- Keep your verbal cues simple, and always use the same one for each exercise. For example, when you ask your puppy to go into the Down position, the cue is "Down", not "Lie Down", Get Down", or anything else... Remember, your dog does not speak English; he associates the sound of the word with the action.

- If your Dachshund is finding an exercise difficult, break it down into small steps so it is easier to understand.

- Do not make your training sessions boring and repetitious; your dog will quickly lose interest.

- Do not train for too long, particularly with a young puppy who has a very short attention span, and always end training sessions on a positive note.

- Above all, have fun so you and your Dachshund both enjoy spending quality time together.

|First lessons

A Dachshund puppy will soak up new experiences like a sponge, so training should start from the time your pup arrives in his new home. It is so much easier to teach good habits rather than trying to correct your puppy when he has established an undesirable pattern of behavior.

Wearing a collar

Most pet dogs wear a collar on a permanent basis, so it is a good idea to get your pup used to wearing one from an early stage. Even though he may not need to wear a collar in the house, he will be on the leash when he goes out in public places, so he needs to get used to the feel of a collar around his neck. The best plan is to accustom your pup to wearing a soft collar for a few minutes at a time until he gets used to it.

- Fit the collar so that you can get at least two fingers between the collar and his neck. Then have a game to distract his attention. This will work for a few moments; then he will stop, put his back leg up and scratch away at the peculiar itchy thing round his neck, which feels so odd.

- Bend down, rotate the collar, pat him on the head and distract him by playing with a toy or giving him a treat. Once he has worn the collar for a few minutes each day, he will soon ignore it and become used to it.

- Remember, never leave the collar on the puppy unsupervised, especially when he is outside in the garden, or when he is in his crate, as it is could get snagged, causing serious injury.

Walking on the lead

- Once your puppy is used to the collar, take him outside into your secure garden where there are no distractions.

- Attach the leash and, to begin with, allow him to wander with the leash trailing, making sure it does not become snagged up. Then pick up the leash and follow the pup where he wants to go – he needs to get used to the sensation of being attached to you.

- The next stage is to get your Dachshund to follow you, and for this you will need some tasty treats. You can show him a treat in your hand, and then encourage him to follow you. Walk a few paces, and if he is co-operating, stop and reward him. If he puts on the brakes, simply change direction and lure him with the treat.

- Next, introduce changes of direction so your puppy is walking confidently alongside you. At this stage, introduce a verbal cue "Heel" when your puppy is in the correct position. You can then graduate to walking your puppy outside the home – as long as he has completed his vaccination program – starting in quiet areas and building up to busier environments.

- Do not expect too much of your puppy too soon when you are leash walking away from home. He will be distracted by all the new sights and sounds he encounters, so concentrating on leash training will be difficult for him. Give him a chance to look and see, and reward him frequently when he is walking forward confidently on a loose leash.

Come when called

Teaching a reliable recall is invaluable for both you and your Dachshund. You are secure in the knowledge that your dog will come back when he is called, and your Dachshund benefits from being allowed off the leash and having the freedom to investigate all the exciting new scents he comes across.

The Dachshund likes to be with his people, but he is a scenthound and the drive to investigate new scents and follow a trail can be overpowering. At these times, a Dachshund will become 'deaf' to your calls, and this can be very frustrating, so much so that you may be reluctant to allow your dog off-leash.

This is counter productive as a Dachshund needs the opportunity to exercise, and restricting his freedom will seriously impinge on his quality of life. You need to work at recalls, providing high value rewards, so your Dachshund wants to come back to you.

- The breeder may have started this lesson, simply by calling the puppies to "Come" at mealtimes, or when they are moving from one place to another.

- You can build on this when your puppy arrives in his new home, calling him to "Come" when he is in a confined space, such as the kitchen. This is a good place to build up a positive association with the verbal cue – particularly if you ask your puppy to "Come" to get his dinner!

- The next stage is to transfer the lesson to the garden. Arm yourself with some treats, and wait until your puppy is distracted. Then call him, using a higher-pitched, excited tone of voice. At this stage, a puppy wants to be with you, so capitalize on this and keep practicing the verbal cue, and rewarding your puppy with a treat and lots of praise when he comes to you.

- Now you are ready to introduce some distractions. Try calling him when someone else is in the garden, or wait a few minutes until he is investigating a really interesting scent. When he responds, make a really big fuss of him and give him extra treats so he knows it is worth his while to come to you. If your puppy responds, immediately reward him with a treat.   If he is slow to come, run away a few steps and then call again, making yourself sound really exciting. Jump up and down, open your arms wide to welcome him; it doesn't matter how silly you look, he needs to see you as the most fun person in the world.

- When you have a reliable recall in the garden, you can venture into the outside world. Do not be too ambitious to begin with; try a recall in a quiet place with the minimum of distractions, and only progress to more challenging environments if your Dachshund is responding well.

- Do not make the mistake of only asking your dog to come at the end of a walk. What is the incentive in coming back to you if all you do is clip on his leash and head for home? Instead, call your dog at random times throughout the walk, giving him a treat and a stroke, and then letting him go free again. In this way, coming to you is always rewarding, and does not signal the end of his free run.

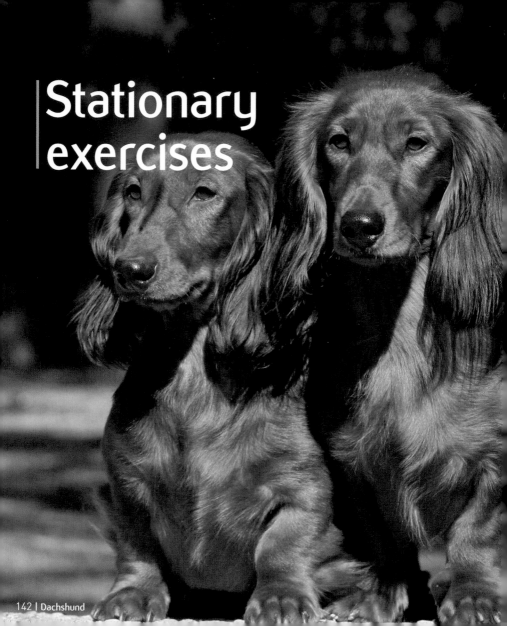

Stationary exercises

The Sit and Down are easy to teach, and mastering these exercises will be rewarding for both you and your Dachshund.

Sit

The best method is to lure your Dachshund into position, and for this you can use a treat, a toy, or his food bowl.

- Hold the reward (a treat or food bowl) above his head. As he looks up, he will lower his hindquarters and go into a sit.

- Practice this a few times and when your puppy understands what you are asking, introduce the verbal cue "Sit".

- When your Dachshund understands the exercise, he will respond to the verbal cue alone, and you will not need to reward him every time he sits. However, it is a good idea to give him a treat on a random basis when he co-operates to keep him guessing!

Down

This is an important lesson, and can be a lifesaver if an emergency arises and you need to bring your Miniature Schnauzer to an instant halt.

- You can start with your dog in a Sit or a Stand for this exercise. Stand or kneel in front of him and show him you have a treat in your hand. Hold the treat just in front of his nose and slowly lower it towards the ground, between his front legs.

- As your Dachshund follows the treat he will go down on his front legs and, in a few moments, his hindquarters will follow. Close your hand over the treat so he doesn't cheat and get the treat before he is in the correct position. As soon as he is in the Down, give him the treat and lots of praise.

- Keep practicing, and when your Dachshund understands what you want, introduce the verbal cue "Down".

Control
exercises

These exercises are not the most exciting, but they are useful in a variety of different situations. It also teaches your Dachshund that you are someone to be respected, and if he co-operates, he is always rewarded for making the right decision.

Wait

This exercise teaches your Dachshund to "Wait" in position until you give the next command; it differs from the Stay exercise, in which he must stay where you have left him for a more prolonged period. The most useful application of "Wait" is when you are getting your dog out of the car and you need him to stay in position until you clip on his leash.

- Start with your puppy on the leash to give you a greater chance of success. Ask him to "Sit" and stand in front him. Step back one pace, holding your hand, palm flat, facing him. Wait a second and then come back to stand in front of him. You can then reward him and release him with a word, such as "OK".

- Practice this a few times, waiting a little longer

before you reward him, and then introduce the verbal cue "Wait".

- You can reinforce the lesson by using it in different situations, such as asking your Dachshund to "Wait" before you put his food bowl down.

Stay

You need to differentiate this exercise from the Wait by using a different hand signal and a different verbal cue.

- Start with your dog in the Down; this position is more comfortable for the long-backed Dachshund, so he is more likely to stay put. Stand by his side and then step forwards, with your hand held back, palm facing the dog.

- Step back, release him, and then reward him. Practice until your Dachshund understands the exercise and then introduce the verbal cue "Stay".

- Gradually increase the distance you can leave your puppy, and increase the challenge by walking around him – and even stepping over him – so that he learns he must "Stay" until you release him.

Leave

A response to this verbal cue means that your Dachshund will learn to give up a toy on request, and it follows that he will give up anything when he is asked, which is very useful if he has a forbidden object. You can also use it if you catch him red-handed raiding the bin, or digging up a prized plant in the garden.

Some Dachshunds can be a little possessive over toys, and some think that running off with a 'trophy' is the greatest fun. This may appear to be harmless, but if your let your Dachshund get away with it, he will think he has the upper hand and may start to take advantage in other situations. It is therefore important to teach your puppy that if he gives up something, he will get a reward, which may be even better than the object he had in the first place!

- The "Leave" command can be taught quite easily when you are first playing with your puppy. As you gently, take a toy from his mouth, introduce the verbal cue, "Leave", and then praise him.

- If he is reluctant, swap the toy for another toy or a treat. This will usually do the trick.

- Do not try to pull the toy from his mouth if he refuses to give it up, as they will only make him keener to hang on to it. Let the toy go 'dead' in your hand, and then swap it for a new, exciting toy, so this becomes the better option.

- Remember to make a big fuss of your Dachshund when he co-operates. If he is rewarded with verbal praise, plus a game with a toy or a tasty treat, he will learn that "Leave" is always a good option.

Play a game of swap so your Dachshund does not become possessive with his toys.

Opportunities for Dachshunds

The Dachshund is a highly intelligent dog, and with positive training he will achieve good results. If you have ambitions to try more advanced training or compete in one of the canine disciplines, he will be a willing pupil.

Good citizen scheme

The Kennel Club Good Citizen Scheme was introduced to promote responsible dog ownership, and to teach dogs basic good manners. In the US there is one test; in the UK there are four award levels: Puppy Foundation, Bronze, Silver and Gold.

Exercises within the scheme include:

- Walking on leash

- Road walking

- Control at door/gate.

- Food manners

- Recall

- Stay

- Send to bed

- Emergency stop.

Competitive obedience

This is a sport where you are assessed as a dog and handler, completing a series of exercises including heelwork, recalls, retrieves, stays, sendaways and scent discrimination.

The Dachshund is more than capable of competing in this discipline, but make sure training is fun, and you do not put too much pressure on your dog. The Obedience exercises are relatively simple to begin with, involving heelwork, a recall and stays in the lowest class, and, as your progress through, more exercises are added, and the aids you are allowed to give are reduced.

To achieve top honors in this discipline requires intensive training, as precision and accuracy are of paramount importance. However, you must guard against drilling your Dachshund, as he will quickly lose motivation.

Rally O

If you do not want to get involved in the rigors of Competitive Obedience, you may find that a sport called Rally O is more to your liking.

This is loosely based on Obedience, and at the highest level it has a few exercises borrowed from agility. Handler and dog must complete a course, in the designated order, which has from 12 to 20 different exercises. The course is timed and the team must complete within the limit that is set, but there are no bonus marks for speed.

The great advantage of Rally O is that it is very relaxed, and anyone can compete; indeed, it has proved very popular for handlers with disabilities, as they are able to work their dogs to a high standard and compete on equal terms.

Tracking

The Dachshund is a scenthound and so tracking is a challenge that he thoroughly enjoys. In organized tracking events, dogs must learn to follow scent trails of varying age, over different types of terrain. These become increasingly tough as a dog works his way through the levels. The greatest honor is to become a Tracking Champion.

Agility

It has to be said that the Dachshund does not really have the conformation to compete in Agility, but, surprisingly, there are a few that prove the doubters wrong. In competition, each dog completes the course individually and is assessed on both time and accuracy. The dog that completes the course with the fewest faults, in the fastest time, wins the class. The obstacles include an A-frame, a dog-walk, weaving poles, a seesaw, tunnels, and jumps.

Earthdog trials

The American Kennel Club runs earthdog trials, which are specifically designed to test the working ability of dogs that were bred to "go to ground" in search of quarry. Man-made tunnels are created, and the dog must work the tunnels in order to find the quarry, which he will indicate by barking, whining, scratching or digging. The quarry (usually two rats) are protected by wooden bars across the end of the tunnel so they are not endangered. The Dachshund is a highly enthusiastic competitor in this sport and performs with distinction.

Showing

If you plan to exhibit your Dachshund in the show ring, you will need to be a dedicated groomer – or employ the services of a professional – to ensure that your dog looks his best when he is inspected by the judge.

You will also need to spend time training your Dachshund to perform in the show ring. A dog that does not like being handled by the judge, or one that does not walk smartly on the lead, is never going to win top honors, even if he is a top-quality animal. To do well in the ring, a Dachshund must have that quality that says: "look at me!", proving he is a real showman.

In order to prepare your Dachshund for the busy show world, you need to work on his socialization, and then take him to ringcraft classes so you both learn what is required in the ring.

Showing at the top level is highly addictive, so watch out – once you start, you will never have a free date in your diary!

Health care

We are fortunate that the Dachshund is a healthy dog and, with good routine care, a well-balanced diet, and sufficient exercise, most will experience few health problems.

However, it is your responsibility to put a program of preventative health care in place – and this should start from the moment your puppy, or older dog, arrives in his new home.

Vaccinations

Dogs are subject to a number of contagious diseases. In the old days, these were killers, and resulted in heartbreak for many owners. Vaccinations have now been developed, and the occurrence of the major infectious diseases is now very rare. However, this will only remain the case if all pet owners follow a strict policy of vaccinating their dogs.

There are vaccinations available for the following diseases:

Adenovirus: This affects the liver; affected dogs have a classic 'blue eye'.

Distemper: A viral disease which causes chest and gastro-intestinal damage. The brain may also be affected, leading to fits and paralysis.

Parvovirus: Causes severe gastro enteritis, and most commonly affects puppies.

Leptospirosis: This bacterial disease is carried by rats and affects many mammals, including humans. It causes liver and kidney damage.

Rabies: A virus that affects the nervous system and is invariably fatal. The first sign is abnormal behavior, when the infected dog may bite another animal or a person. Paralysis and death follow. Vaccination is compulsory in most countries. In the UK, dogs traveling overseas must be vaccinated.

Kennel Cough: There are several strains of Kennel Cough, but they all result in a harsh, dry, cough. This disease is rarely fatal; in fact most dogs make a good recovery within a matter of weeks and show few signs of ill health while they are affected. However, kennel cough is highly infectious among dogs that live together so, for this reason, most boarding kennels will insist that your dog is protected by the vaccine, which is given as nose drops.

Lyme Disease: This is a bacterial disease transmitted by ticks (see page 169). The first signs are limping, but the heart, kidneys and nervous system can also be affected. The ticks that transmit the disease occur in specific regions, such as the north-east states of the USA, some of the southern states, California and the upper Mississippi region. Lyme disease is still rare in the UK so vaccinations are not routinely offered.

Vaccination program

In the USA, the American Animal Hospital Association advises vaccination for core diseases, which they list as distemper, adenovirus, parvovirus and rabies.

The requirement for vaccinating for non-core diseases – leptospirosis, lyme disease and kennel cough – should be assessed depending on a dog's individual risk and his likely exposure to the disease.

In the UK, vaccinations are routinely given for distemper, adenovirus, leptospirosis and parvovirus.

In most cases, a puppy will start his vaccinations at around eight weeks of age, with the second part given a fortnight later. However, this does vary depending on the individual policy of veterinary practices, and the incidence of disease in your area.

You should also talk to your vet about whether to give annual booster vaccinations. This depends on an individual dog's levels of immunity, and how long a particular vaccine remains effective.

Parasites

No matter how well you look after your Dachshund, you will have to accept that parasites – internal and external – are ever present, and you need to take preventative action.

Internal parasites: As the name suggests, these parasites live inside your dog. Most will find a home in the digestive tract, but there is also a parasite that lives in the heart. If infestation is unchecked, a dog's health will be severely jeopardized, but routine preventative treatment is simple and effective.

External parasites: These parasites live on your dog's body – in his skin and fur, and sometimes in his ears.

Roundworm

This is found in the small intestine, and signs of infestation will be a poor coat, a pot belly, diarrhoea and lethargy. Pregnant mothers should be treated, but it is almost inevitable that parasites will be passed on to the puppies. For this reason, a breeder will start a worming program, which you will need to continue. Ask your vet for advice on treatment, which will need to continue throughout your dog's life.

Tapeworm

Infection occurs when fleas and lice are ingested; the adult worm takes up residence in the small intestine, releasing mobile segments (which contain eggs) that can be seen in a dog's feces as small rice-like grains. The only other obvious sign of infestation is irritation of the anus. Again, routine preventative treatment is required throughout your Dachshund's life.

Heartworm

This parasite is transmitted by mosquitoes, and so will only occur where these insects thrive. A warm environment is needed for the parasite to develop, so it is more likely to be present in areas with a warm, humid climate. However, it is found in all parts of the USA, although its prevalence does vary. At present, heartworm is rarely seen in the UK.

Heartworm live in the right side of the heart. Larvae can grow up to 14in (35.5cm) in length. A dog with heartworm is at severe risk from heart failure, so preventative treatment, as advised by your vet, is essential. Dogs living in the USA should have regular blood tests to check for the presence of infection.

Lungworm

Lungworm, or *Angiostrongylus vasorum*, is a parasite that lives in the heart and major blood vessels supplying the lungs. It can cause many problems, such as breathing difficulties, blood-clotting problems, sickness and diarrhoea, seizures, and can even be fatal. The parasite is carried by slugs and snails, and the dog becomes infected when ingesting these, often accidentally when rummaging through undergrowth.

Common
ailments

Dogs can be affected by a variety of ailments, most of which can be treated effectively after consulting with your vet, who will prescribe appropriate medication and will advise you on how to care for your dog's needs.

Here are some of the more common problems that could affect your Dachshund, with advice on how to deal with them.

Anal glands

These are two small sacs on either side of the anus, which produce a dark-brown secretion that dogs use when they mark their territory. The anal glands should empty every time a dog defecates but if they become blocked or impacted, a dog will experience increasing discomfort. He may nibble at his rear end, or 'scoot' his bottom along the ground to relieve the irritation.

Treatment involves a trip to the vet, who will empty the glands manually. It is important to do this without delay or infection may occur.

Dental problems

Vets report that dental problems are becoming increasingly common among the dog population, and can cause serious discomfort. However, good dental hygiene will do much to minimize gum infection and tooth decay. If tartar accumulates to the extent that you cannot remove it by brushing, the vet will need to intervene. In a situation such as this, an anesthetic will need to be administered so the tartar can be removed manually.

Diarrhoea

There are many reasons why a dog has diarrhoea, but most commonly it is the result of scavenging, a sudden change of diet, or an adverse reaction to a particular type of food.

If your dog is suffering from diarrhoea, the first step is to withdraw food for a day. It is important that he does not dehydrate, so make sure that fresh drinking water is available. However, drinking too much can increase the diarrhoea, which may be accompanied with vomiting, so limit how much he drinks at any one time.

After allowing the stomach to rest, feed a bland diet, such as white fish or chicken with boiled rice, for a few days. In most cases, your dog's motions will return to normal and you can resume normal feeding, although this should be done gradually.

However, if this fails to work and the diarrhoea persists for more than a few days, you should consult you vet. Your dog may have an infection which needs to be treated with antibiotics, or the diarrhoea may indicate some other problem which needs expert diagnosis.

Ear infections

The Dachshund has drop ears that lie close to the head. This means that air cannot circulate as freely as it would in a dog with semi-pricked or pricked ears, so it is important to keep a close check on your Dachshund's ears.

A healthy ear is clean with no sign of redness or inflammation, and no evidence of a waxy brown discharge or a foul odor. If you see your dog scratching his ear, shaking his head, or holding one ear at an odd angle, you will need to consult your vet.

The most likely causes are ear mites, an infection, or there may a foreign body, such as a grass seed, trapped in the ear.

Depending on the cause, treatment is with medicated ear drops, possibly containing antibiotics. If a foreign body is suspected, the vet will need to carry our further investigations.

Eye problems

The Dachshund has medium-sized eyes, set obliquely in the skull. They do not protrude – which is important, as breeds with prominent eyes, such as the Pekingese, are vulnerable to injury.

If your Dachshund's eyes look red and sore, he may be suffering from conjunctivitis. This may, or may not be accompanied with a watery or a crusty discharge. Conjunctivitis can be caused by a bacterial or viral infection, it could be the result of an injury, or it could be an adverse reaction to pollen.

You will need to consult your vet for a correct diagnosis, but in the case of an infection, treatment with medicated eye drops is effective.

Conjunctivitis may also be the first sign of more serious inherited eye problems (see page 184). In some instances, a dog may suffer from dry, itchy eye, which he may make worse through scratching. This condition, known as keratoconjunctivitis sicca, may be inherited.

Foreign bodies

In the home, puppies – and some older dogs – cannot resist chewing anything that looks interesting. The toys you choose for your dog should be suitably robust to withstand damage, but children's toys can be irresistible. Some dogs will chew – and swallow – anything from socks, tights, and any other items from the laundry basket to golf balls and stones from the garden. Obviously, these items are indigestible and could cause an obstruction in your dog's intestine, which is potentially lethal.

The signs to look for are vomiting, and a tucked up posture. The dog will often be restless and will look as though he is in pain. In this situation, you must get your dog to the vet without delay as surgery will be needed to remove the obstruction.

Heatstroke

The Dachshund's head structure is without exaggeration, which means that he has a straightforward respiratory system, and does not suffer breathing problems experienced by flat-nosed breeds, such as the Pug or the French Bulldog.

However, all dogs can overheat on hot days, and this can have disastrous consequences. If the weather is warm, make sure your Dachshund always has access to shady areas, and wait for a cooler part of the day before going for a walk. Be extra careful if you leave your Dachshund in the car, as the temperature can rise dramatically - even on a cloudy day. Heatstroke can happen very rapidly, and unless you are able lower your dog's temperature, it can be fatal.

If your Dachshund appears to be suffering from heatstroke, lie him flat and work at lowering his temperature by spraying him with cool water and covering him with wet towels. As soon as he has made some recovery, take him to the vet where cold intravenous fluids can be administered.

Facing page: Take special care of your Dachshund when the temperature rises.

Lameness/limping

There are a wide variety of reasons why a dog can
go lame, from a simple muscle strain, to a fracture,
ligament damage, or more complex problems with
the joints. The Dachshund's conformation, with his
elongated back, means that spinal problems may
occur. You need to be so be extra vigilant, making
sure your Dachshund is moving freely, as well
avoiding exercise which could put an undue strain on
his back. If you are concerned about your dog, do not
delay in seeking help.

As your Dachshund becomes more elderly, he may
suffer from arthritis, which you will see as general
stiffness, particularly when he gets up after resting.
It will help if you ensure his bed is in a warm draft-
free location, and if your Dachshund gets wet after
exercise, you must dry him thoroughly.

If your Dachshund seems to be in pain, consult your
vet, who will be able to help with pain relief medication.

Skin problems

If your dog is scratching or nibbling at his skin, first
check he is free from fleas (see page 168). There are
other external parasites which cause itching and hair
loss, but you will need a vet to help you find the culprit.

An allergic reaction is another major cause of skin problems. It can be quite an undertaking to find the cause of the allergy, and you will need to follow your vet's advice, which often requires eliminating specific ingredients from the diet, as well as looking at environmental factors.

can occur in one or both ears. In the UK, the Kennel Club no longer registers puppies from two dapple parents.

Endocrine disorders

There may be an increased risk of:

Hypothyroidism: An under-active thyroid resulting in an altered metabolism. There are many symptoms including lethargy, intolerance to exercise and weight gain. Hormone replacement therapy is generally effective.

Cushing's Disease: Caused by an excess of corticosteroid hormones, it often occurs in older dogs. Signs include weight gain, increased thirst, and increased urine output. Medical treatments are available.

Diabetes Mellitus: A metabolic disorder that results in increased thirst and increased urine output. There are a number of treatments options available depending on the type of diabetes.

Eye disorders

In the US, the Canine Eye Registration Foundation (CERF) was set up by dog breeders concerned about heritable eye disease, and provides a database of dogs that have been examined by diplomates of the

American College of Veterinary Ophthalmologists. In the UK, there are Kennel Club/British Veterinary Association schemes in place to test for particular eye conditions.

The Dachshund may be affected by the following:

Distichiasis

This occurs in the Miniature Long-haired Dachshund where there is an extra row of eyelashes, which rub on the cornea. Surgery is required in severe cases.

Entropion

This is an in-turning of the eyelids, which has varying degrees of severity. In the most serious cases, surgical correction is required because of the pain and damage inflicted on the surface of the eyeball.

Generalised progressive retinal atrophy (GPRA)

GPRA is a bilateral degenerative disease of the cells (rods and cones) of the retina, leading initially to night blindness and progressing to complete loss of vision. Dogs are affected from three to four years of age and there is no cure. There is a test available for younger dogs, before being used for breeding, to prevent carrier individuals passing on the genetic defect.

Optic nerve hypoplasia

This occurs in Miniature Long-haired Dachshunds, and involves the failure of the optic nerve to develop, resulting in blindness. Testing is available.

Other inherited conditions

Intervertebral disc disease (IVDD)

This affects the discs located between the Dachshund's spine. There are different types; the Dachshund's short, thick limbs means that he is predisposed to Type 1 IVDD. The signs may first appear in dogs aged from four to seven years and are characterized by severe pain, weakness, and loss of bladder control. If left untreated, permanent paralysis may occur. Surgical treatment is often successful.

Lafora's disease

This occurs in Miniature Wire-haired Dachshunds; onset is from five years onwards. It is a form of epilepsy caused by a specific gene mutation. A DNA test is now available.

Mitral valve disease

This is a heart condition in which blood leaking through the mitral valve can be heard as a murmur when a dog is examined with a stethoscope. Signs include intolerance to exercise, coughing and breathlessness and, at worst, heart failure may result. Treatment will depend on the severity of the case.

Summing up

It may give the pet owner cause for concern to find about health problems that could affect their dog. But acquiring some basic knowledge is an asset, as it will allow you to spot signs of trouble at an early stage. Early diagnosis is very often the means to the most effective treatment.

Fortunately, the Dachshund is a generally healthy and disease-free dog with his only visits to the vet being annual check-ups. In most cases, owners can look forward to enjoying many happy years with this affectionate and highly entertaining companion.

Useful addresses

Breed & Kennel Clubs
Please contact your Kennel Club to obtain contact information about breed clubs in your area.

UK
The Kennel Club (UK)
1 Clarges Street London, W1J 8AB
Telephone: 0870 606 6750
Fax: 0207 518 1058
Web: www.thekennelclub.org.uk

USA
American Kennel Club (AKC)
5580 Centerview Drive, Raleigh, NC 27606.
Telephone: 919 233 9767
Fax: 919 233 3627
Email: info@akc.org
Web: www.akc.org

United Kennel Club (UKC)
100 E Kilgore Rd, Kalamazoo,
MI 49002-5584, USA.
Tel: 269 343 9020
Fax: 269 343 7037
Web:www.ukcdogs.com/

Australia
Australian National Kennel Council (ANKC)
The Australian National Kennel Council is the administrative body for pure breed canine affairs in Australia. It does not, however, deal directly with dog exhibitors, breeders or judges. For information pertaining to breeders, clubs or shows, please contact the relevant State or Territory Body.

International
Fédération Cynologique Internationalé (FCI)
Place Albert 1er, 13, B-6530 Thuin, Belgium.
Tel: +32 71 59.12.38
Fax: +32 71 59.22.29
Web: www.fci.be/

Training and behavior
UK
Association of Pet Dog Trainers
Telephone: 01285 810811
Web: http://www.apdt.co.uk

Canine Behaviour
Association of Pet Behaviour Counsellors
Telephone: 01386 751151
Web: http://www.apbc.org.uk/

USA
Association of Pet Dog Trainers
Tel: 1 800 738 3647
Web: www.apdt.com/

American College of Veterinary Behaviorists
Web: http://dacvb.org/

American Veterinary Society of Animal Behavior
Web: www.avsabonline.org/

Australia
APDT Australia Inc
Web: www.apdt.com.au

For details of regional behaviorists, contact the relevant State or Territory Controlling Body.

Activities
UK
Agility Club
http://www.agilityclub.co.uk/

British Flyball Association
Telephone: 01628 829623
Web: http://www.flyball.org.uk/

USA
North American Dog Agility Council
Web: www.nadac.com/

North American Flyball Association, Inc.
Tel/Fax: 800 318 6312
Web: www.flyball.org/

Australia
Agility Dog Association of Australia
Tel: 0423 138 914
Web: www.adaa.com.au/

NADAC Australia
Web: www.nadacaustralia.com/

Australian Flyball Association
Tel: 0407 337 939
Web: www.flyball.org.au/

International
World Canine Freestyle Organisation
Tel: (718) 332-8336
Web: www.worldcaninefreestyle.org

Health
UK
British Small Animal Veterinary Association
Tel: 01452 726700
Web: http://www.bsava.com/

Royal College of Veterinary Surgeons
Tel: 0207 222 2001
Web: www.rcvs.org.uk

Alternative Veterinary Medicine Centre
Tel: 01367 710324
Web: www.alternativevet.org/

USA
American Veterinary Medical Association
Tel: 800 248 2862
Web: www.avma.org

American College of Veterinary Surgeons
Tel: 301 916 0200
Toll Free: 877 217 2287
Web: www.acvs.org/

Canine Eye Registration Foundation
The Veterinary Medical DataBases
1717 Philo Rd, PO Box 3007,
Urbana, IL 61803-3007
Tel: 217-693-4800
Fax: 217-693-4801
Web: http://www.vmdb.org/cerf.html

Orthopaedic Foundation of Animals
2300 E Nifong Boulevard
Columbia, Missouri, 65201-3806
Tel: 573 442-0418
Fax: 573 875-5073
Web: http://www.offa.org/

American Holistic Veterinary Medical
Association
Tel: 410 569 0795
Web: www.ahvma.org/

Australia
Australian Small Animal Veterinary
Association
Tel: 02 9431 5090
Web: www.asava.com.au

Australian Veterinary Association
Tel: 02 9431 5000
Web: www.ava.com.au

Australian College Veterinary Scientists
Tel: 07 3423 2016
Web: http://acvsc.org.au

Australian Holistic Vets
Web: www.ahv.com.au/